CONTENTS

HOW TO WRITE A RESEARCH PAPER MADE EASY

CHAPTER 1
Introduction

Research can sound like a big scary word.

But it's really just finding out what you need to know by asking questions.

Who do you ask?

That depends on the question.

If my question is, "What happens when baking soda and vinegar mix?" the best way to find out might be to mix baking soda and vinegar.

Or, I could watch someone else do it online.

If my question is, "Where's the best place to get my car fixed?" I might ask friends and family members (who have cars) where they get their cars fixed, and whether they're satisfied with what was done. I might look online for reviews of shops.

If my question is, "When's the best time to plant strawberries in my garden?" I might ask someone in my neighborhood who grows strawberries or someone at the nearest store that sells strawberry plants. Or, I might look it up online (But I'd have to be careful to get a time that works for my neighborhood. It doesn't matter how good the advice is for Boston if I live in Houston.)

If my question is, "How did America change after 9-11?" the best way might be to ask a lot of people who were in America both before 9-11 and afterward. Then I could use their answers to form my own opinion.

Or, I could read books and articles that ask people this question.

Or, I could read books and articles that give opinions about this.

In all these cases, research is just answering a question. To research, I ask a question and then answer it by making an experiment, asking people who know the answer, or finding the information in print or online.

Then what?

Often, (for example, when I'm looking for the best car repair shop or the best time to plant strawberries in my neighborhood), once I've found my answer, I act on it, and then I'm done. I take my car to the shop, or I plant my strawberries.

But, for school, often I need to write what I've found in a paper or display it in some kind of project. In school, (and sometimes at work) research involves not just asking a question and finding the answer, but also presenting that answer to others.

CHAPTER 2
Understand the Assignment

Most people write research papers because someone tells them to. That is, they have an assignment. Usually, that assignment is for a class. Sometimes it's for a job. Sometimes a teacher tells students about the assignment, but usually it will also have written instructions. They might look something like this:

SAMPLE 1
For an English Class:

Choose a poet from this list and write a 10-page paper that explores the interaction between that poet's life and their work. Be sure to include excerpts from at least three poems, and reference at least three biographical sources. Use MLA format for documentation.

*Maya Angelou * Conrad Aiken * Elizabeth Bishop ** *Gwendolyn Brooks * e e cummings * Stephen Crane* * Emily Dickinson * Paul Laurence Dunbar * Hilda* *Doolittle * T S Eliot * Ralph Waldo Emerson ** *Robert Frost * Langston Hughes * Oliver Wendall* *Holmes * Helen Hunt Jackson * Joyce Kilmer ** *Henry Wadsworth Longfellow * Vachel Lindsay* * Amy Lazarus * Audre Lorde * Claude McKay* * Marianne Moore * Edna St. Vincent Millay ** *Ogden Nash * Edgar Allen Poe * Dorothy Parker* * Sylvia Plath * Ezra Pound * Carl Sandburg **

*Wallace Stevens * Anne Sexton * Gertrude Stein*
** Sara Teasdale * Walt Whitman * Ella Wheeler*
*Wilcox * Elinor Wylie * William Carlos Williams*
** Phyllis Wheatly * John Greenleaf Whittier*

First Draft Due: April 7

Teacher Conferences Available (attend at least one): April 7, 8, 9, 12, 14, 15

Second Draft Due: April 14

Final Draft Due: April 16

SAMPLE 2
For a History Class:

Vietnam War Presentations: For our next project, you will give a 3-5 minute presentation on a Vietnam War topic. Be sure to get your topic approved before you begin your research. You will also need to turn in a bibliography that includes at least 5 sources, 3 or more of them primary sources, documented in MLA style. Sign up for a presentation time on the sheet in the front of the classroom. Grading will be based 60% on content (organization, historical analysis, use of sources) and 40% on the presentation (oral skills, posture, gestures, and visual aids).

SAMPLE 3
For a Science Class:
Choose one ocean-based animal species that is affected by climate change. Your group of four will create either a website or a Google Slides presentation that reports about this animal or plant species and how it is affected. Be sure to include informa-

tion about the animal's important characteristics, life cycle, diet, lifestyle, and habitat. Cite at least 4 sources, using APA. Presentations and time to look at websites will be in class September 17 and 19.

Handling Assignments

When I get an assignment like this, it can feel like a lot, but most assignments answer some or all of the same questions:

- ❖ What should I research?
- ❖ How many sources (and what kinds of sources) do I need?
- ❖ What format do I need to use to show what sources I used?
- ❖ What does my report/presentation need to look like?
- ❖ What is (or are) the deadline (deadlines)?
- ❖   What other things should I think about as I do this assignment?

We'll look at these questions one at a time.

What should I research?

If I turn in an essay about Taylor Swift for any of the topics above, no matter how well-researched and well-written the essay is, it will almost certainly fail. Why? Because it doesn't match the assignment. How can I find what I should research? I look for words like "choose," "on," or "about" and see what the assignment says after that. It's a good idea to also look for "make sure," "be sure to" or "include." In our sample questions, we had:

CHOOSE a poet from this list

ON a Vietnam War topic

CHOOSE one ocean-based animal species that is affected by climate change. INCLUDE information ABOUT the animal's important characteristics, life cycle, diet, lifestyle, and habitat

These kinds of phrases limit what topics are available for this assignment.

How many sources (and what kinds of sources) do I need?

Many research assignments will say how many sources are needed. Look for the words "source," "cite," or "bibliography." In our samples, we had:

include excerpts from at least three poems, and reference at least three biographical SOURCES. (This is probably at least four sources--three for the bio-graphical information, one or more for the poems.)

turn in a BIBLIOGRAPHY that includes at least 5 sources, 3 or more of them primary sources

CITE at least 4 SOURCES

We'll talk much more about this later, but it's good to remember when you're counting sources, that encyclopedias (whether on-line or in a library) do not count as a source.

What format do I need to use to show what sources I used?

Many assignments will say what form of documentation to use. A few will assume that students already know what to use (for example, if a school always uses MLA format for all classes, then the teachers may not feel like they have to tell people this.) Usually, to find this information, look for the word "format," or "style" or look for common formats (MLA, APA, Chicago, Turabian). In our samples, we have:

Use MLA FORMAT for documentation

documented in MLA STYLE

using APA

What does my report/presentation need to look like?

Research is often reported in a paper of a given length. If an assignment wants me to write a paper, it will often have the word "paper," but it may say, "report," "essay," "argument," or "analysis." These are all papers. To know how long a paper should be, I look for "words" or "pages." Sometimes research is presented orally or in some kind of project (media presentation; computer game; poster; map) instead. In these cases, the type of project will probably be listed, and there may be information about how long (in minutes) a presentation should be. Sometimes, reporting on research involves both a project AND a paper. I always watch for words like "and" and "or." These tell me if I have to turn in two things--or if I can choose one of two (or several) ways to report my research. In our samples, we had:

a 10-PAGE PAPER

a 3-5 minute PRESENTATION, a BIBLIOGRAPHY, VISUAL AIDS (notice, for this research, students will give a speech AND turn in a bibliography, or list of the sources they used. "Visual Aids" came from the part that said how the presentation would be graded.)

a WEBSITE OR a GOOGLE SLIDES PRESENTATION (In this assignment, the students will only do one of these things. They could create a website. Or, if they'd rather, they could make a slide presentation.)

What is (or are) the deadline (deadlines)?

Knowing when an assignment should be turned in is important. It helps me plan my research and writing. Often, I just look for the word "due." If the word "due" is not in the assignment, I look for dates. Sometimes, instead of an exact date, there's a "sign up," and I'll find my due date when I sign up. In our samples, we had:

The following due dates are all for the SAMPLE 1. Some teachers want to see a paper several times before the final is turned in: First Draft DUE: April 7; Teacher Conferences Available (attend at least one): April 7, 8, 9, 12, 14, 15; Second Draft DUE: April 14; Final Draft DUE: April 16

The due dates for SAMPLE 2 may be different for every student. The sign-up form will tell me when my presentation is due: SIGN UP for a presentation time on the sheet in the front of the classroom.

For SAMPLE 3, students probably need to be finished by September 17th: Presentations and time to look at websites will be in class SEPTEMBER 17 AND 19.

What other things should I think about as I do this assignment?

Sometimes assignments include other important information. For example, SAMPLE 2 has this sentence: "Be sure to get your topic approved before you begin your research." Often when teachers let students pick their topics, they want the students to talk with them about whether their topic will work out or not. They don't want students to do lots of work on something that may not fit the assignment or may be too difficult to research.

SAMPLE 2 also tells students how the assignment will be graded. Often teachers will give this information to help students know what the teacher expects from them. To find this kind of information, look for words like "grading" or "rubric."

GRADING will be based 60% on content (organization, historical analysis, use of sources) and 40% on presentation (oral skills, posture, gestures, and visual aids).

Sometimes research is done by more than one student. In SAMPLE 3, this is the case. To find this kind of information, look for words like "pair," or "partner," or "group."

your GROUP of four

Make a Checklist

Once I've looked through an assignment to make sure I understand all the things I should do, I often make a checklist that I can go through before turning in my paper or project. With my checklist, I can make sure I don't forget anything important for the assignment.

My checklist could be a set of questions, or it could be a set of statements.

For example, for SAMPLE 1, I might make the following checklist:

❖ *Did I choose a poet from the list?*

❖ *Does my paper talk about how the poet's life*

affected their poetry?

- ❖ *Do I have at least 3 biographical sources?*
- ❖ *Did I format my citations in MLA?*
- ❖ *Is my paper at least 10 pages long?*
- ❖ *Did I finish my first draft by April 7?*
- ❖ *Did I have a conference with the teacher?*
- ❖ *Did I finish my second draft by April 14?*
- ❖ *Did I finish my final draft by April 16?*

For SAMPLE 2, I might make this checklist:

- ❖ Vietnam War topic
- ❖ Topic approved by teacher
- ❖ Signed up for presentation time
- ❖ 5 or more sources
- ❖ 3 or more primary sources
- ❖ Bibliography in MLA
- ❖ Visual Aids
- ❖ Practiced
- ❖ 3-5 minutes
- ❖ Presentation Date: December 11

For SAMPLE 3, my group might make this checklist:

- ❖ *Google Slides or website?*
- ❖ *Ocean-based animal species that is affected by climate change?*
- ❖ *4 sources?*
- ❖ *APA?*
- ❖ *Characteristics?*
- ❖ *Life-cycle?*

- ❖ *Diet?*
- ❖ *Lifestyle?*
- ❖ *Habitat?*
- ❖ *Ready by September 17?*

WORKING WITH OTHERS

Working with the teacher:

If there's something I'm not sure about, this is a great time to ask teachers questions about what they expect. I like to ask these questions in class because if I'm not sure about something, there are probably other students who are also confused. If, for some reason, I don't feel comfortable asking the teacher questions in front of everyone else, I usually try asking after class or during office hours.

Working with a tutor or writing center:

A tutor can help me look at an assignment and make sure I understand it.

Working with friends or other students:

Other students in the same class may also be glad to talk with me about what they think the assignment wants us to do. If we all think the assignment means the same thing, probably that's what it means. If we disagree about what the assignment means, it's probably a good idea to ask the teacher to explain a bit more.

CHAPTER 3
Choose a Topic

Often, I get to choose what to write about. Sometimes I don't. Whenever I get to choose, I like to keep two main things in mind:

1. I choose a topic that interests ME (so you should choose a topic that interests YOU). I do better, more fun research if I like my topic. It's likely that my paper or project will be better, too.
2. Choose a topic that fits the assignment.

It can also be good to choose a topic that isn't exactly the same as the topic lots of other people are doing.

Sometimes it's hard to find a topic that is interesting and fits the assignments, but if I can do it, everything else will be better.

The following 4-step process can help

1. Brainstorm topics that will fit the assignment
2. Make the list of topics smaller
3. Learn about the topics on the smaller list
4. Choose one topic

Step 1: Brainstorm Topics that will Work with the Assignment

Often, the first idea I think of for a topic isn't the one that will interest me most. That's why I often start by thinking of as many topics as I can that will fit the assignment. That way, there's a higher chance that one of them will be interesting. If I can't think of any topics (or I can only think of one or two), I might do a quick web search or look in a textbook or encyclopedia to get some ideas (yes, at this point, looking in Wikipedia is OK!). If I struggle with English, but have no trouble in another language, this might be a good time to use textbooks or encyclopedias in the other language to quickly learn what I need to know. Here's how it looks in our sample assignments:

SAMPLE 1:

This step is already included in the assignment. We can choose one of the poets from this list:

*Maya Angelou * Conrad Aiken * Elizabeth Bishop * Gwendolyn Brooks * e e cummings * Stephen Crane * Emily Dickinson * Paul Laurence Dunbar * Hilda Doolittle * T S Eliot * Ralph Waldo Emerson * Robert Frost * Langston Hughes * Oliver Wendall Holmes * Helen Hunt Jackson * Joyce Kilmer * Henry Wadsworth Longfellow * Vachel Lindsay * Amy Lazarus * Audre Lord * Claude McKay * Marianne Moore * Edna St. Vincent Millay * Ogden Nash * Edgar Allen Poe * Dorothy Parker * Sylvia Plath * Ezra Pound * Carl Sandburg * Wallace Stevens * Anne Sexton * Gertrude Stein * Sara Teasdale * Walt Whitman * Ella Wheeler Wilcox * Elinor Wylie * William Carlos Williams * Phyllis Wheatly * John Greenleaf Whittier*

Note: In a case like this, where the teacher asks students to choose from a list, if I don't like any of the topics in the list, I might look for something that I would like that is closely related. (in this case, another American poet)

SAMPLE 2:

I don't know much about the Vietnam War, so to get good topics on this one, I need to learn something. After looking at the Vietnam War Wikipedia page, I'm able to make this list:

*Kennedy * Johnson * The Tet Offensive * Media
* the Draft * Draft Dodgers * African Americans
in the war * Nurses * Napalm * War Crimes *
Low Tech vs High Tech (Bicycles vs. Bombers)
* Women in the War * Amerasians*

I could keep going, but I already see a couple of topics on here that I might be interested in, so I will stop.

SAMPLE 3:

This is another one where I need to look up topics that might fit. After putting "ocean animals affected by climate change" into a search engine, I was able to find some articles that helped me start a list:

*plankton * corals * copepods * marine turtles * damselfish * cardinal fish * summer flounder * sea lions...*

More time could probably create a much larger list.

Once I have a list, if I see a topic that sounds super interesting, I could choose it (for example, in Sample 1, I already know I love Gwendolyn Brooks, and I could stop here, and go to the next chapter. If I'm not sure yet which of my topics might be interesting, I can move on to step 2.

Step 2: Make the List Smaller

If I didn't immediately love one of the ideas in step one, the next step is to make the list smaller. We can do this in a number of ways. One is by crossing out items I don't like for one reason or another. Another is by thinking about things I'm interested in and seeing if any of the topics from Step 1 connect with any of these things. The important thing in this step is to make the list smaller by taking out (or keeping in) the topics that are most likely to be interesting or fun (for the person doing the research. In the examples below, I'm showing how *I'd* make the list of topics shorter based on what **I** like, but when it comes time for **YOU** to do **YOUR** research, it's very important for you to think about what **YOU** like and don't like, not what I like and don't like. Or what your best friend likes and doesn't like. Or even what your teacher likes and doesn't like--though if your teacher has said there's a particular topic he or she hates, it might be good to avoid that one.)

SAMPLE 1:

Crossing Out: I like modern writers, so I can cross out all the poets on this list who were born before 1900.

Maya Angelou * ~~Conrad Aiken~~ * Elizabeth Bishop * Gwendolyn Brooks * e ~~e cummings~~ * ~~Stephen Crane~~ * ~~Emily Dickinson~~ * ~~Paul Laurence Dunbar~~ * ~~Hilda Doolittle~~ * ~~T S Eliot~~ * ~~Ralph Waldo Emerson~~ * ~~Robert Frost~~ * Langston Hughes * ~~Oliver Wendall Holmes~~ * ~~Helen Hunt Jackson~~ * ~~Joyce Kilmer~~ * ~~Henry Wadsworth Longfellow~~ * ~~Vachel Lindsay~~ * ~~Amy Lazarus~~ * Audre Lorde * ~~Claude McKay~~ * ~~Marianne Moore~~ * ~~Edna St. Vincent Millay~~ * Ogden Nash * ~~Edgar Allen Poe~~ * ~~Dorothy Parker~~ * Sylvia Plath * ~~Ezra Pound~~ * ~~Carl Sandburg~~ * ~~Wallace Stevens~~ * Anne Sexton * ~~Gertrude Stein~~

~~Sara Teasdale~~ *~~Walt Whitman~~* *~~Ella Wheeler Wilcox~~* *~~Elinor Wylie~~* *~~William Carlos Williams~~* *~~Phyllis Wheatly~~* *~~John Greenleaf Whittier~~*

This leaves this much shorter list:

Maya Angelou * *Elizabeth Bishop* * *Gwendolyn Brooks* * *Langston Hughes* * *Audre Lorde* * *Ogden Nash* * *Sylvia Plath* * *Anne Sexton.*

Connections with my interests: Even though this is shorter, it is still eight names. I know I like women writers, and I like African American literature, so I will pick the African American women on this list:

Maya Angelou * *Gwendolyn Brooks* * *Audre Lorde*

This is a list small enough for Step 3

SAMPLE 2:

Crossing Out: I'm not fond of violence, so I would take some violent topics off my list.

Kennedy * *Johnson* * *~~The Tet Offensive~~* * *Media* * *the Draft* * *Draft Dodgers* * *African Americans in the war* * *Nurses in Vietnam* * *~~Napalm~~* * *~~War Crimes~~* * *Low Tech vs High Tech (Bicycles vs. Bombers)* * *Women in the War* * *Amerasians*

This leaves a shorter list, but not much shorter.

Connections with my interests: I like writing and journalism, and I also like hearing about how women and minority groups fit into history, so I might shorten my list to this:

Media * *African Americans in the War* * *Nurses* * *Women in the War* * *Amerasians*

I could move on to Step 3 at this point. This list is a bit big for Step

3, though, so if some of these topics sound more interesting to me than others, I might pick the three that are most interesting:

*Media * Nurses in Vietnam * Amerasians*

Now I'm ready for Step 3

SAMPLE 3:

This topic is tricky, because it is a group project, so you have to consider not only your own interests, but also the interests of others in your group.

Crossing Out: After talking, perhaps your group decides you're most interested in more complex animals, so you cross out all the invertebrates:

*~~plankton~~ * ~~corals~~ * ~~copepods~~ * marine turtles * damselfish * cardinal fish * summer flounder * sea lions*

This leaves a list of only 5, which might be small enough for moving on to Step 3. Or we could decide to pick only the most complex animals on the list, so we're left with marine turtles and sea lions. These are pretty general categories, so I might pick a particular turtle and a particular sea lion: Hawaiian Green Sea Turtle and California Sea Lions as we move on to Step 3.

Step 3: Learn about the topics on the smaller list

Now, I want to learn enough about each topic in my short list that I can tell which one I like best. Again, I can look in an encyclopedia or a textbook or do a basic online search to learn more about each one (This is another time when it is OK to use Wikipedia or the Encyclopedia Britannica, or another source you may not want to cite in your final project).

SAMPLE 1:

If I do a quick search for biographical information and poems for my top three choices, I can learn the following:

Maya Angelou:

1928-2014

in addition to poet, singer, actress, autobiography writer

1 poem https://www.poetryfoundation.org/ poems/48988/awaking-in-new-york

Gwendolyn Brooks:

1917-2000

"The people in the workshops have told me, over and over again, that they had hated poetry because they were forced to memorize it in elementary school and high school, and it was presented as something heavy, to be gotten through for the sake of grades. The thing I am interested in doing is in presenting poetry as a living thing, an instrument of pleasure, of release, and they enjoy it when it's given to them that way." (Conversations by Roy Newquist, 1967)[1];

1 poem https://www.poetryfoundation.org/ poetrymagazine/poems/28110/the-bean-eaters

Audre Lorde:

1934-1992

"black, lesbian, mother, warrior, poet,[2]"

1 poem https://www.poetryfoundation.org/ poems/42582/afterimages

SAMPLE 2:

If I do a quick search for information on my top three topics, I can learn:

Media during the Vietnam War:

Vietnam called "first television War"

*Some people say that reporting made
America lose the war*

Others say reporters acted responsibly

Nurses in the Vietnam War:

*Most of the US military women in Vietnam
were nurses (women were prohibited
from serving in combat roles)*

*Nurses served US soldiers, captured and wounded
Viet Cong soldiers, and Vietnamese civilians*

*Though the women's movement was opening more
careers to women, it was easier for American
women to become nurses than many other careers.*

Amerasians

*Huge numbers of children were born to
Vietnamese mothers and American servicemen
fathers (more than 20,000)*

*These children and their mothers
were discriminated against*

*Many of these children were abandoned
and became orphans*

Some were brought to the US (Operation Babylift)

SAMPLE 3:

If I do a quick search for information on my top topics, I can learn:

Hawaiian Green Sea Turtles:

Beautiful

Endangered

Rising sea levels affect nesting sites

*Warmer seas affect decrease the number
of males born*

California Sea Lions:

Kind of cute

*Climate change made it harder to
feed the pups for a while*

*Sea Lions appear to have adapted to the
warmer oceans; their numbers are back up*

Step 4: Choose one Topic

Pick one topic. Maybe, after Step 3, it's easy to see which topic will be most fun to research. Maybe one topic will seem like a better fit for the assignment than the others. Maybe one topic will seem much easier to research than the others.

If none of these help, and all the topics seem equally good, I could always roll a die, and put the topics I didn't choose into a file for ideas for later (in case I have a future class with an assignment that one of them would fit.)

SAMPLE 1:

When I look at what I learned in Step 3, Maya Angelou's life sounds fascinating; Gwendolyn Brooks's words about poetry make me want to read it more; and Audre Lorde's poem made me cry.

It's a hard choice. I would be interested in any of these. All of them fit the assignment well. They seem equally easy to research.

This might be a good time to use chance. I'm rolling a die. 1 or 2 for Maya Angelou, 3 or 4 for Gwendolyn Brooks, 5 or 6 for Audre Lord. And the answer is: 6.

My topic choice is Audre Lorde.

SAMPLE 2:

When I look at what I learned in Step 3, I find that I got most excited about the last topic, Amerasians, so that is my pick here.

My topic choice is Amerasians.

SAMPLE 3:

When I look at what I learned in Step 3, I think that the turtles will fit the topic better than the sea lions. They are endangered, and climate change is affecting them more.

My topic choice is Hawaiian Sea Turtles.

WORKING WITH OTHERS

Working with the teacher

In Step 1, teachers might be able to give some sample topics that will work with their assignment. At any point, I could ask if a topic I'm considering would fit the assignment.

Working with a tutor or writing center:

A tutor may be able to help me brainstorm ideas or talk with me about which ideas are most interesting to me.

Working with friends or other students:

Other students in the same class will probably be happy to help brainstorm topic ideas--they have to do the same assignment, after all. They may also be willing to talk with me about which ideas are most interesting to me.

CHAPTER 4
Gather Basic Information

Once I have a topic, I will need to know enough about it to be able to ask a good question. So, I should use what I already know, and if I still need to know more, use encyclopedias and results from search engines to get some basic information.

Use What I Already Know

Maybe I have some personal experience with my topic and feel I already know some things I'd like to learn more about.

Maybe I learned enough about this topic in class that I already know some things I'd like to learn more about.

Maybe, when I was learning about topics for Step 3 in choosing a topic, I found some things I want to learn more about.

If any of these things are true, I should probably move on to the next chapter (Ask a research question). If none of these are true, I probably need to gather a bit more basic information about my topic.

Learn Enough to Ask a Question

This time, when I ask about my topic or read about my topic, my goal is to look for questions I have—things I want to know more about. As with Step 3 in finding a topic, I may look at textbooks, encyclopedia articles or results of quick web searches. If these don't give me enough understanding of my topic to think of good questions about it, I may also try to find a few longer articles or books on my topic.

WORKING WITH OTHERS

Working with the teacher:

Sometimes teachers have good ideas for sources I can use to get a good, quick overview of the topic I'm researching.

Working with a tutor or writing center:

A tutor may also have good ideas for places to get a good, quick overview of the topic I'm researching. They may also be able to help me talk about what I've learned and think up questions.

Working with friends or other students:

Other students in the same class may also be able to help talk about what I've learned and think up questions, especially if they are working on the same topic. (If other students in the same class are working on the same topic, I always try to be a little careful. It can be great to share research and ideas, but I don't want my paper or presentation to look exactly like someone else's!)

CHAPTER 5
Ask a Research Question

Research, we said, was finding out what we need to know by asking questions.

What question should we ask?

Sometimes, the assignment tells us what question to ask.

For example, in SAMPLE 1, the assignment says I need to write a paper that: "explores the interaction between that poet's life and their work." This isn't written as a question, but it tells me that I will be writing about how the poet's life affects their poems (and possibly how the poet's poems affect their life). I can put this as a question: How did the poet's life affect their poems? Did the poet's poems affect their life, and if so, how?

If I put my own topic into these questions, they become:

How did Audre Lorde's life affect her poems?
Did her poems affect her life, and if so, how?

These are the questions I will answer with my research.

Similarly, in SAMPLE 3, the assignment says we should report "about this animal or plant species and how it is affected [by climate change.]" I can write this as a question: How is my animal or plant species affected by climate change?"

If I put in my own topic, this question becomes:

How are Hawaiian sea turtles
affected by climate change?

This is the question I will answer with my research.

Sometimes the assignment does not tell us exactly what our research question should be, so we must decide what we'd like to ask about our topic.

In SAMPLE 2, all the assignment says is that I must give my presentation on a Vietnam War topic. Now, I have to decide what I'd like to know about my topic. As I did my background research, I thought of a few questions:

*How many Amerasian children were
born during the Vietnam War?*

*How did the military deal with soldiers
who fathered Amerasian children?*

*What happened to Amerasians born during
the Vietnam War?*

*How did Amerasians affect the relationship
between the US and Vietnam?*

When I look at these questions to decide which to use, the first thing I'll think about is--will the answer to this question be complicated enough to make into an interesting report (or in this case, 3-5 minute presentation.) The answer to my first question is just a number, so that won't work. The answer to the second question may also be a bit too simple, so I think it would be best to focus on one of the last two questions.

In deciding between these two, I'll think about several things:

*Which question is most interesting to me? They
both are interesting to me, so this is no help.*

*Which question will be easiest to find information
about? There are lots and lots of articles on
the third, so it will be easy to research. If
I'm short on time, that's the way to go.*

Are any of these questions that not many others

are asking? The fourth question is one that hasn't been written about as much--which means it will be harder to research, but my answers may add something to the conversation. This becomes more and more important the farther into college and graduate school I go. If this is for an upper level course, or one where the teacher is looking for unique, new perspectives, I may want to use question four as my research question.

For this book, I'm going to use the third question, because I am a bit short on time, so my research question is:

What happened to Amerasians born during the Vietnam War?

WORKING WITH OTHERS

Working with the teacher:

Sometimes teachers are willing to help me write my research question (especially if the assignment suggests the research question.) Even if they're not, they may be willing to tell me whether they think my research question is a good one. This is something I'd ask them about before or after class or during office hours instead of during the full class.

Working with a tutor or writing center:

A tutor will usually be willing to help me write my research question if I am having trouble coming up with one.

Working with friends or other students:

Other students in the same class may also be able to help talk about what I've learned and think up questions, especially if they are working on the same topic. (If other students in the same class are working on the same topic, we might want to make sure we're not using the exact same research question. This will help our reports or presentations to be different.)

CHAPTER 6

Find Sources of Information

What is a source?

A source is someone or something that has the information I want to know.

A source could be a person.

A source could be written information--a book or article (either in print or online).

A source could be some other media--a picture, map, cartoon, graph, podcast, video or other media.

Not all sources are equally good sources for my research. I need to find sources that are both *reliable* and *relevant*.

Choosing Reliable Sources

A reliable source is one that I can trust to give me accurate information about a topic. Not all sources are reliable.

When I'm thinking about how reliable a source is, I'm going to ask myself questions like:

1. Does this source (or the person/ group who created this source) have enough experience and education to

know what they are talking about?

Once I was talking to a three-year-old boy whose family was expecting a younger sibling, and he told me that he knew how babies were born--they grew in their mother's tummies, and then the doctor cut them out with a big knife. This might be all a three-year-old needs to know about where babies come from if his mother is going to have a c-section. However, if I were having a baby, I would not want to use this child as a source of information about what birth is like. He hadn't seen a birth or studied births in school. He couldn't read to get more information on his own, and the information he had been told was incomplete at best.

I don't want to use sources like that when I'm doing research.

How can I find sources with the experience and education to be reliable?

A. Find out about the source or the author(s) of the source.

What education and experience does this person have?
For example, if I'm working on SAMPLE 1, and considering using the biography *Warrior Poet: A Biography of Audre Lorde* by Alexis De Veaux, I can learn that the author was the head of the Women's Studies Department at the University of Buffalo. I can also learn that Alexis De Veaux and Andre Lorde had met, though they may not have been good friends. That's enough education and experience that I can probably trust this source.

B. Look for primary sources.

A *primary source* is someone (or a record of some sort that is made by someone) who has first-hand experience with your topic. For example, in SAMPLE 2, if I meet someone who is Amerasian, that person could be a primary source for my paper. Similarly, if my grandpa has a buddy who fathered a kid while he was a soldier in Vietnam, that buddy would be a first-hand source. Other primary sources might be journals written by Amerasians or their parents or newspaper articles written about Amerasians moving to the US in 1982, when the US first started bringing Vietnamese American Amerasians into the country. In scientific research, primary sources are reports of experimental research.

C. Look for articles in academic journals that are "peer reviewed."
Before they are published, all the articles in these journals get sent to experts to make sure that they are accurate. This kind of source will be easier to find in a database of peer-reviewed journals like EBSCO Academic Premier or JSTOR than in a general Google search. I can get access to collections like these from a library (usually a university library, though some high school and public libraries may also give me access to them).

D. Look at reviews of the source if they are available.
A number of reviews of *Warrior Poet: A biography of Audre Lorde* mention how well researched it is.

2. Does this source (or the person/ group who created this source) usually tell the truth?

When I was young, we had a family friend who would tell stories about hunting and fishing trips he'd been on, and every time he told us about this deer he shot, or that fish he caught, it was bigger than the last time he'd told the story. Our friend was NOT a reliable source of information about the size of the animals and fish he caught.

I don't want to use sources like that when I'm doing research.

How can I find sources that usually tell the truth?

A. Look for organizations that many people trust:

For example, most universities, some government agencies (like the CDC), some journalism agencies (like AP and Reuters). These groups want people to trust them, so they do their best to make sure that all the information they publish is reliable. Many of these groups will do fact checking as part of their editing process before they publish articles.

For SAMPLE 3, I have found articles about sea turtles from National Geographic, a well-known and highly respected magazine. This is probably reliable information. I also found an article put out by the National Oceanic and Atmospheric Administration. This US government agency keeps records on the environment, puts out alerts about natural disasters (like hurricanes), and helps other government agencies plan for long-term changes. This also is probably reliable information.

B. Look at other things by the author (or group) writing this source.
Do the things they say make sense together, or do some of the things they say contradict other things they say (like my family friend's fish stories)?

3. How recent is this source (when was it published)?

When I was young, my mother used to say that goods made in Japan always fell apart easily. Maybe they did when she was a child, but the time I was around, cars and machines made in Japan were known for their high quality--they almost never fell apart. My mom's information on this might have been true at one time, but it wasn't true anymore.

I don't want to use sources that are so out of date that they're no longer true.

How can I make sure my sources are giving accurate information for today?

If my topic is not historical, it's best if most of my sources come from the past few years. Even if my topic is historical, my secondary sources should be from the past few years. Books can often be a bit older than articles since the books take longer to publish. Since the article mentioned above from the National Oceanic and Atmospheric Administration was published in 2010, it might be best not to use this source.

4. What financial, political, religious, or other opinions does this source (or

the person/group who created this source) have that might affect the way they present information?

When I was a kid, sometimes my sister and I would get into an argument and make a mess or break something. My mother would always have us come to her together, and then one at a time tell her what happened. Usually, what my sister said happened was not exactly what I said happened. Why? Partly because we experienced the fight from our own particular point of view. Also, we each were trying to make ourselves look as good as possible so that we would get in the least trouble. Usually, after hearing both me and my sister, and asking us more questions, my mother was able to get a very good idea of what happened.

Just as my sister and I had different perspectives on what happened when we argued, every source on a research topic comes from one person (or group of people), and so it will be affected by that person's opinions and experiences and by what will be best for that person or group. This is bias. All sources have some bias. I must use sources with bias because every source has some kind of bias.

How can I avoid sources that are so biased that it's hard to recognize the truth?
A. When I'm researching, it can be good to do what my mother did-- make sure to get more than one person's opinion.
If several people with very different biases say the same thing, it is more likely to be true.

B. It may also be good to learn enough about a source to know what kinds of bias it is likely to have.
If I do this, I may be able to guess how a source's bias might be affecting it.

C. If a source's bias is unusually large, I might not want to use that source in my research.

For example, if I were writing a paper about the health effects of smoking, I might not want to use a tobacco company's website as one of my main sources.

Choosing Relevant Sources

When I'm researching, a source is only useful if it can answer my research question. An encyclopedia article that tells all about climate change in the oceans will not (probably) have a lot of information about Hawaiian sea turtles. A textbook chapter that overviews the Vietnam War may mention Amerasians, but it probably won't give enough detail for me to learn what happened to most of them. A book on the Harlem Writer's Guild might mention Audre Lorde, but it probably won't have enough information for me to get a good idea of her poems or life.

How can I find relevant sources?

1. If I know someone who is an expert on this topic, I should definitely ask them if I can interview them.
2. I should look for sources that answer my question as specifically as possible.
3. I can look in the bibliographies of more general books and articles on my topic, to see what references they used to answer my question.
4. When I'm looking in search engines (whether general ones like Google or more specific ones in academic databases), I can use very specific search terms.

   For example, for SAMPLE 1, I can use "Audre Lorde poems" and "Audre Lorde biography" (but I would only put those quotation marks in there if I want the search engines to return results with all three words together in exactly that order.)

   For SAMPLE 2, I can use "Vietnam Amerasian" (see the note above about quotation marks)

For Sample 3, I can use "Hawaiian Sea Turtle Climate Change" (see the note above about quotation marks)

5. If my original search terms don't get me what I want, I can change them until I find what I'm looking for.

6. If I have the chance to go to an actual library, I can find one or two good books about this topic and then go to the section of the library that holds those books. Chances are, I will find other useful books near the ones I found by using the catalog. Some libraries' online catalogs will allow you to do this on your computer. They have a setting that lets you look at the books that would be on the same shelf as a book you think is useful.

7. If I find an article or book that does a great job answering my research question, I should look in its bibliography for other sources that might help.

Use Sources Responsibly

When I was in the fourth grade, my class was working on an art project where we were making snowmen, and I had an idea for how to make a special hat for my snowman. The girl next to me saw me make this hat, and she thought it was great, so she made one just like it. That felt wonderful. Then the teacher came over and saw the other girl's snowman hat and showed the whole class. The teacher said it was a great idea, and she thought the other girl was very smart. The other girl did not say that she got the idea from me. I felt very angry. I felt like the other girl was stealing my idea.

In the US, originality—new ideas—are very important. If I suggest that a set of words (or a new way to do things or a photograph) is mine when I copied it from someone else, I'm likely to be accused of stealing that picture or idea or those words. In US schools, stealing others' words (also called *plagiarism*) is serious.

If a teacher finds that I've copied the work of another student or that I've used words, facts, and original ideas from an expert without saying where those words come from, I could get a bad grade on the assignment, fail a course, or even get kicked out of school.

On the other hand, we expect people to use the words, facts, and ideas of experts to support their arguments when they write research papers. So how do I do this without getting people angry with me? I make sure that when I use material from sources outside my brain, I *document* where the material came from. This does two things. First, it makes my argument stronger by letting people know that this material isn't just my idea; it comes from an expert. Second, it shows that I am not claiming the material as my own. I am not stealing the material, just using it to help explain or support my own ideas.

Of course, when I do this, I must make sure that the material I am using really does explain or support my own ideas. No one likes to have their own words used to support ideas and arguments that they disagree with.

Document Sources

There are a number of different systems for documenting sources, but they all help readers know how to find the sources I use to answer my research question in case they (the readers) are interested in finding out more on their own--or in case they want to make sure what I've told them about the source is correct.

Often, the different systems will put a small amount of information in the body of the report. For example, the words may mention the author, the date of publication or the title. Some systems have me put some information about a source in parenthesis right after I've used material from that source. Others will put a footnote or endnote after the material.

Footnotes and endnotes often include more information, than parenthetical notation. In many systems there is also a list of

"Works Cited" or "References" at the end of the report that lists all the sources.

In general, documentation will usually tell the following information about a source (if this information can be found):

- ❖ The author
- ❖ The date of publication (and/or date the source was accessed if it is online)
- ❖ A link to the source (if it is online)
- ❖ The page number where the quote or other material was found (if it is printed)
- ❖ The publisher or periodical title, volume, and issue number
- ❖ Place of Publication
- ❖ The title of the book, article, or essay

Documentation will also sometimes tell

- ❖ The edition
- ❖ The editor (for collections of essays or other works by multiple authors)
- ❖ The series title (for books in a series)
- ❖ The translator

Different systems put this information in different orders, so it's important to know what system my assignment requires me to use. Many schools have one style that they use; other schools will let each department choose which style to use for documentation. If I'm not sure what my assignment requires, I should ask.

For example, here are a couple of the sources I mentioned in "Choose Reliable Sources" documented two different ways. These two styles are NOT the only ways to document sources, they are just two commonly used examples.

APA

In APA, in the text, if write about a general idea or to the whole work, I use parenthesis with the author name, a comma, and the date of publication. If I directly quote or paraphrase the material, I will also include a page number. If I name the author or date in the sentence, I only put the information I have not written in the parenthesis.

(De Veaux, 2004, p. 200)

(Welch, 2019)

At the end of my paper, in APA, I will have a page that lists more information about all of my sources. It will look like this:

References

De Veaux, A. (2004). *Warrior Poet: A Biography of Audre Lorde.* W. W. Norton & Company Inc.

Welch, C. (2019, April 4). Sea turtles are being born mostly female due to warming—will they survive: Climate change is causing a crisis in sea turtle sex ratio. But there are signs of hope. *National Geographic Website.* Retrieved from https://www.nationalgeographic.com/environment/2019/04/sea-turtle-sex-ratio-crisis-from-climate-change-has-hope/

MLA

In MLA, in the text, I use parenthesis with the author name and page number (or paragraph number) of the quote or other material unless I've used the author name in my writing, in which case, I put only the page number:

(De Veaux 200)

(Welch par. 8)

At the end of my paper, in MLA, I will have a page that lists more information about all of my sources. It will look like this:

Works Cited

De Veaux, Alexis. *Warrior Poet: A Biography of Audre Lorde*. W. W. Norton & Company Inc., 2004, New York.

Welch, Craig. "Sea turtles are being born mostly female due to warming--will they survive: Climate change is causing a crisis in sea turtle sex ratio. But there are signs of hope." *National Geographic Website.* 4 Apr. 2019. www.nationalgeographic.com/environment/2019/04/sea-turtle-sex-ratio-crisis-from-climate-change-has-hope/. Accessed 30 May 2020.

WORKING WITH OTHERS

Working with a librarian:

Often, if I'm having difficulty finding sources that will answer my research question, a librarian can help me. Librarians are good at using search engines to find sources, and they have great ideas on how to get started. In many libraries, I can look for a librarian and ask my questions, and they'll help. Sometimes I need to make an appointment with a librarian to get specific help on a research project.

Working with a tutor or writing center:

A tutor may be willing to help me locate reliable and relevant sources for my research.

Working with friends or other students:

If other students in my class are working on topics similar to mine, there may be sources they're using that would also answer my research question—or sources I'm using that could also answer their research question. In that case, sharing sources could be great. Also, if I come across a topic that doesn't answer my research question, but does answer my classmates,' I might send them a link or the name of the source. It doesn't take me much time, and they might do the same for me.

CHAPTER 7

RESEARCH

Interview Experts

If I know an expert in my topic who is willing to let me interview them, that's a wonderful source. I will want to set up a time and place to meet that is convenient for them (and possible for me). It might help everyone to relax if we meet somewhere like a coffee shop or some other place where we can eat and drink (and I'd expect to pay for the other's food and drink), but if that doesn't work for them, I wouldn't push it. I'd try to do what makes the other person comfortable and what fits in their schedule.

When I set up the appointment, I might ask if they mind if I record the interview, so I know whether that's possible.

Before I meet with them, I will write a list of questions I want to ask them. I may think of other questions I want to ask during the interview, but this beginning list will at least help me get started. I will try to ask questions that can't be answered by reading books, webpages, and articles.

If the other person will let me record the interview, I will. That way, while I'm interviewing them, I can pay attention to what they're saying and ask follow-up questions.

Even if I have a recorder, I will also take some notes on paper--I never know when a recording might not work properly. If I cannot record, it is extra important to take good notes.

For most things, I will try to write only the big ideas that the person says, but if they say something I want to quote, I might repeat it back to them to make sure I heard them correctly.

On my notes, for documentation, I'll write down the name of the person I'm interviewing and the place and time that we met.

Read to Answer a Research Question

Many times, when I'm researching, I don't know any people who can answer my questions. In that case, I will look for books, articles and other media that will answer my question.

Using this reading to create a good research paper or project means taking good notes. Notes can be used for lots of different purposes.

Notes for understanding

I can take notes to make sure I understand. Often, after reading an article, I will outline it or summarize it to make sure that I understand what it is about. For example, for the National Geographic article I mentioned earlier, I might write the following summary:

> *Camryn Allen, a researcher with the National Oceanic and Atmospheric Administration, uses blood samples to find out which baby sea turtles are female and which are male. She found that in Raine Island, Australia, "female baby turtles now outnumber males 116 to 1" (Welch, 2019, par. 5) Baby sea turtles are already at risk from microbes and predators. Humans also threaten turtle habitats and kill turtles on accident and for commerce. All this worries Allen. However, other researchers have discovered that in some sea turtle populations, males are now mating with multiple females, which may help the population survive. In addition, techniques like planting trees to cool down sand may also help reverse some of the turtle feminization trends.*

Summarizing what I've read helps me know that I understood it fully. I can do the same thing by outlining an article, book chapter, or other important information. If I can restate what I read, I feel confident that I understand it.

Notes to develop an opinion

When I take notes to understand, I'm mostly repeating what someone else thinks. To develop my own thoughts, I might write a bit about what I've read. For example, I might write something like this:

> *It seems like climate change is warming the sands, making more baby sea turtles female than they used to be, but climate change isn't the only thing making life tough for sea turtles. They're also facing habitat loss, which in this article appears to be coming from people moving onto beaches rather than from rising seas (climate change). Living close to people and getting caught in boat propellers is also taking a toll, as is human hunting (so the turtle shells are used for jewelry and whatnot.) Sea turtles are in danger from humans, but it's not just a climate change issue (though climate change is part of it.)*

Notes to remember important details

If there's an important quote or fact I want to remember, I could highlight it (if I have a copy of the article or book that I can mark up) or I could take notes to make sure I remember this quote or fact--and that I remember how to document it.

> *She found that in Raine Island, Australia, "female baby turtles now outnumber males 116 to 1" (Welch, 2019, par. 5)*

Notes to find information again

With my other notes, I always want to keep information about how I'll document this source. I hate it when I have a great statistic or quote that I found for a paper--and I've lost the documentation. When that happens, I either spend hours looking it up again or can't use it in my research. So frustrating.

To keep this from happening, I like to keep all my notes for one research project in a single notebook. I'll start a new source on a new page, put the documentation at the top, then include a summary and any quotes or facts I might want later, and finally my reaction to these things below that. For people who prefer to keep all their work on a computer, they can do the same thing in a single research document.

Some people prefer to use index cards because once they have the information they want, they can easily move it around into the order that makes most sense for their paper of project. That's great as long as they make sure that every card has some way to show what source the information on it came from.

For the article I've been taking notes on in this section, here's the full documentation:

Welch, C. (2019, April 4). Sea turtles are being born mostly female due to warming--will they survive: Climate change is causing a crisis in sea turtle sex ratio. But there are signs of hope. National Geographic Website. *Retrieved from https:// www.nationalgeographic.com/environment/2019/04/sea-turtle-sex-ratio-crisis-from-climate-change-has-hope/*

WORKING WITH
OTHERS

I usually find it difficult to work from others notes, but sometimes it can help to share work, especially if I need to find dozens of sources for a research project, and there are others working on the same project--or similar ones. Nobody else can take notes on my reactions to things, but if others are good at writing summaries and finding important quotes, facts and figures, we could divide up a huge list of sources and exchange notes. When I see others' summaries of articles and books that might be useful for me, I can more quickly decide which are the most worth the time it takes to read them carefully myself.

CHAPTER 8
Write a Thesis Statement

The heart of my research paper or project will be a thesis statement. A good thesis statement will answer the research question. A good thesis statement will help others understand something they might not have understood before about my topic. A good thesis statement will be something that I'll need to explain and argue for. Usually, I won't know what my thesis statement is until after I have done my research.

Example Thesis Statements:

SAMPLE 1: Audre Lorde's political activism as an African American lesbian feminist shows up as angry, but powerful language in her poetry.

SAMPLE 2: The Amerasians born during the Vietnam War are people without a country: accepted by neither their Asian nor their American home countries.

SAMPLE 3: Though not the only threat Hawaiian green sea turtles face, climate change endangers the creatures in a variety of ways.

WORKING WITH OTHERS

Once I have written a thesis statement, it can often be helpful to have someone else—a teacher, a tutor, a friend or a fellow student—look at that statement and tell me if they think it's too hard to understand or too obvious. Often, I cannot tell these things very well myself.

CHAPTER 9

Outline

Before starting to write, many people find it helpful to write an outline to organize their thoughts. Some people are very formal about this, using Roman numerals and letters. Others may give more of a list of which topics to cover in what order.

For the Sea Turtle paper, a partial outline might look something like this:

❖ Though not the only threat Hawaiian green sea turtles face, climate change endangers the creatures in a variety of ways.
  ➤ Feminization of baby sea turtles (warming sands)
    · National Geographic article (Allen study)
    · Global Change biology article (Patricio study)
    · Current Biology Study (Jenson et al study)
    · Science Total Environment (Bell et al study)
  ➤ Habitat loss (sea level rise)

WORKING WITH OTHERS

Unless I must work with a group on my paper, I usually write outlines by myself. However, if I am working with a group, writing an outline is a great way to organize the project at the beginning and decide who should create which pieces of the project.

CHAPTER 10
Draft

This is easy to explain, and sometimes hard to do. Once I have my research, my thesis statement, and maybe an outline, I need to write the paper.

I put myself in a chair with my writing tools in front of me and write.

Sometimes I'll write directly into a computer. In fact, right now, with this book, I'm writing this way. Lots of people only write this way.

Sometimes, though, I like to write with a paper and pencil because the feel of the pencil in my hand helps me think. Lots of people think this is weird. It's a slow process because once I have my thoughts on paper, I have to type them into a computer, but if I have enough time, I will often write this way.

I have friends who like to write using a speech-to-text application. That is, they have an app that lets them talk into their computer or phone, and the computer or phone changes what they say into writing. For some of my friends, who can talk more easily than they can write, this is a good way to get text to work with.

I also have met people who feel more comfortable writing in a language other than English who will write papers in that language first and then translate them. This can be slow, and can lead to awkward English, but it can also be an effective way of getting ideas into a report.

If I try writing my paper one way, and I get stuck, often I will switch to something else for a while to see if that works better for me.

WORKING WITH
OTHERS

Unless I'm working in a group, I usually don't write WITH other people. If I AM writing in a group, usually the group and I divide the paper or other project into sections and assign different sections to different people to write. Then I write my sections.

CHAPTER 11
Revise

Organize

Once I have my paper or speech (or website) written, I want to make sure that the writing makes sense. One of the first things to do is to make sure the writing is organized. If I didn't write an outline for my paper before my first draft, now might be a good time to do it, because, often it's easier to see problems with organization in outlines than in whole papers.

To check my organization, I may ask myself questions like:

Do all the paragraphs support my thesis?
For example, in SAMPLE 2, if my thesis is that Amerasians have been treated unfairly by both their Asian countries and the US, but I have a paragraph that talks about how it's relatively easy for Amerasians to immigrate to the US, I might need to do some work to show how this does not contradict my thesis.

Does each paragraph have ideas that belong together?
For example, in SAMPLE 3, if I have information about sea level rise affecting nesting sites, that should be in a different paragraph from information about warmer water affecting how many baby turtles are female.

Strengthen Arguments
Usually a research paper or project is made up of arguments that all tie together to convince the reader or listener (or watcher)

that my thesis statement is true.

When I'm reading through my paper, I want to make sure that each argument is strong. Usually that means that the argument has three parts:

1. A clear statement of what I am arguing:

For example, "Climate change endangers Hawaiian green sea turtles by feminizing baby turtles."

2. Evidence that this statement is true:

For example, "Warmer sands cause more of the sea turtles to be born female."

3. Logic that explains how the evidence proves what I am arguing:

For example: "Climate change makes sands warmer, warmer sands means a higher percentage of female baby sea turtles are born, that means a lower percentage of male baby sea turtles are born, which means, over time, there will be fewer adult male sea turtles, which means fewer mating sea turtle pairs, which eventually means fewer sea turtles."

Usually, in English we find it important to spell out all three parts of the argument--the statement, the evidence, and the explanation of how the evidence proves the statement. Sometimes this last part (the explanation) is so obvious that people feel they don't need to include it, but it is better to include it when it's not needed than to need it and not have it.

To make sure I have a strong research paper, I'll want to make sure that every argument in my paper does a good job of parts one and two—stating what I'm arguing and providing enough evidence to convince people this argument is true. Often, I'll also want to make sure my arguments include the third part also--the explanation of how my evidence supports my arguments.

Make it Easy to Understand
When I'm writing, sometimes I know exactly what I mean, but

when somebody else reads the words, they think, "What?"

This is an area where it's very helpful to get input from another person, but if I don't have someone else who can ask me about things they don't understand, I might find it useful to leave the paper or project alone for a few hours (a few days is even better). When I return to the paper and read it again, it may be easier for me to notice things that aren't explained very well.

I might also look through the paper for e sentences that go on and on and on. Long sentences with lots of clauses are difficult to write clearly.

Use Great Transitions

It is easiest to understand papers where there are good connections between the paragraphs. I'll want to check each place where there is a new paragraph to make sure there is some word, phrase, or idea that links the paragraph before it to the new one.

I can always use transitional words like first, second, then, next. It might be even better to use a sentence that picks up an idea from the previous sentence and then points toward the ideas for the new paragraph. For example, I might say "In addition to feminizing baby sea turtles, climate change is reducing sea turtle habitat."

Polish Introductions and Conclusions

Introductions and conclusions are important because they give the first and last impression of my project.

An introduction always needs some kind of "hook"--something that will get the reader interested in the paper. This could be a story or an interesting quote or a shocking fact. The introduction might also include some background information on the topic. Then the introduction needs to give my thesis statement.

Conclusions, of course, need to help the reader understand that everything has ended. Usually they will give some sort of summary of what I have discovered in my research. Often they will use different words to restate the thesis statement. Sometimes they will point toward new research that this project has made me wish I could do.

WORKING WITH OTHERS

Working with a teacher:
Many teachers will give feedback on early drafts of papers. If a teacher is collecting first drafts, I always make sure to have my draft finished in time for the teacher to give me comments. I also try to pay attention to what the teacher has said and to fix the problems a teacher has noticed because they're the one who will be grading my paper.

Working with a tutor or writing center:
A tutor or writing center can often help me notice problems with organization, weak arguments, unclear language, transitions, introductions, and conclusions and help me think of ways to make these problems better. I like to take teacher feedback to a writing center when I can because that also helps the tutors there understand what my teacher wants. I may not always change my paper when a tutor or writing center says I should, but most of the time I do.

Working with friends or other students:
It's great to get others' opinions of my writing because other people notice things I don't. Sometimes, though, when a friend

or another student reads my work they say, "that was great," even if it wasn't. Other times, friends and fellow students give me advice that seems wrong. I find it helps to ask specific questions: What parts (if any) were difficult to understand? Where might it have been helpful to add more information? Which sections (if any) seemed out of place? Then, I carefully think about what my friends or classmates have said. Usually, if they point out a problem, I need to do something about it, even if the thing they suggest that I do is not a good idea for my paper.

Whatever a teacher, tutor, friend or classmate tells me is worth listening to—but sometimes their advice isn't the best thing for my paper. I may feel that my paper is better the way it is. Or I may feel that the problem they found is worth fixing, but the way they think I should fix it is not the best thing. It's my paper, so I need to decide what advice to take and what advice to ignore.

CHAPTER 12
Edit

Once I have the content of my paper in good shape, it's time to clean up all the picky little problems that might be there. Some of these will be caught by a good grammar and spell checker, so I should definitely use these tools. Spell checkers and grammar checkers will not catch everything, though, so I need to read through my papers on my own as well. If I know I have particular grammar issues, I should spend time focusing on these.

Verb Tenses and Agreement

If I have trouble with verb tenses and agreement, I may want to go through my paper and highlight every verb in it. I can do this with a highlighter in my word processor, or I can do it with a highlighting pen on a paper copy. Then I should treat my paper like a grammar exercise and make sure every one of those verbs has the form I want it to have.

Run-ons and Fragments

A sentence has a subject and a verb, and it expresses a complete thought.

Run-ons

If I put two sentences together without appropriate punctuation or conjunctions, this is called a run-on. Lots of people use run on sentences. They're easy to fix, though. I can fix the run-on by (1) joining the sentences with a word like "and" or "but" **along with** a comma; (2) Splitting the run-on into two sentences; (3) joining the sentences with a semicolon, a word like "however" and a comma; OR (4) making one of the sentences dependent on the other by adding a word like "since" or "when."

For example:

"The turtles won't be able to keep mating there will be no males left." Is a run-on sentence because "The turtles won't be able to keep mating" is a sentence, and so is "there will be no males left."

Ways to fix it:

1. The turtles won't be able to keep mating, for there will be no males left.

2. The turtles won't be able to keep mating. There will be no males left.

3. There will be no males left; therefore, the turtles won't be able to keep mating.

4. The turtles won't be able to keep mating because there will be no males left.

Fragments

If I put a period after one of those dependent clauses, it's still not a sentence because it doesn't express a complete thought. This is a fragment. Fragments can be confusing because they're meant to connect with something, but don't. For example, "when the sands get hotter" is a fragment. It's begging me to answer the question "What happens when the sands get hotter?" Fragments can often be fixed by joining them to the sentence before or after them. If that doesn't work, a fragment might need a new sentence to hang onto. Alternatively, the fragment can be turned into a sentence by taking off the beginning word (the "when" or "since" or "because" or "if").

Instead of "When the sands get hotter" I can write:

*When the sands get hotter, more of
the turtles are born female.*

OR

The sands get hotter.

Prepositions

Prepositions aren't usually big problems for native speakers of English, but for non-native speakers, sometimes it's hard to remember which prepositions go with which other words. Unfortunately, there aren't good rules for this. It's one of those things that just have to be memorized. (Why do we say endangered by instead of endangered with? No reason, we just do.)

To make sure prepositions are right in a paper, the best thing to do is have a native speaker look at the paper and tell me when they notice prepositions are off. Another non-native speaker may also find problems I don't notice. If I don't have a friend who can help me, I can highlight prepositions in the same way I highlighted verbs earlier.

Articles

Correctly using articles (the, an, a) is another grammar issue that isn't usually a big problem for native speakers of English but can be troublesome for non-native speakers.

The definite article (the) is used whenever both I and my reader know exactly which thing (or things) I am writing about. For example, I write "the sun" because there's only one sun. If I've mentioned something the sentence before, I'll use "the" the next time I use it because the reader and I will both know I mean the one I just mentioned. If I describe something very clearly, I may also use the (the beaches of Raine Island in Australia).

Indefinite articles (a and an) are used with singular countable nouns that aren't definite. If the thing could be any one of many things, I will use "a" or "an"--a young turtle needs to get to the sea without being eaten by a predator.

Every time I have a singular (just one) countable noun, I have to use some kind of article. Plural nouns (like pens) or uncountable nouns (like love) only need articles if they're definite (both the reader and I know exactly which ones we're talking about).

To make sure articles are right in a paper, the best thing to do is have a native speaker look at the paper and tell me when they notice missing or incorrect articles. Another non-native speaker may also find problems I don't notice. If I don't have a friend who can help me, I can highlight every noun and check to see if there is an appropriate article (or lack of article) in front of it.

Formatting References

Some teachers care a lot about references having every period and comma in the right place, so it's good to make sure all my documentation is done correctly.

Final Read Through

Before I turn a paper in, it's always good to read it through one last time. It's amazing how many mistakes and problems I can catch this way.

To catch even more mistakes, I may read it aloud.

It might also be a good idea to take one last look at the checklist I made back when I was working on understanding my assignment, just to make sure I have done all the things I need to.

WORKING WITH OTHERS

Working with a teacher:

Some teachers will mark every typo and grammar error in an early draft of a paper, but many teachers won't. If my teacher does this, I try to pay attention to what they've marked, and make a mental list of what kinds of mistakes I make. Chances are, I'll make the same kinds of mistakes on future papers--and that will help me know what to look for when I'm editing.

Working with a tutor or writing center:

A tutor or writing center employee can often help me locate grammatical errors, but I may have to ask them specifically to do this.

Working with friends or other students:

Just as it's great to get help revising, it's also great to get others' help with editing because other people notice things I don't. If I have a friend who is particularly good at finding typos, or fixing mistakes with articles, or putting in commas when I forget them, they're a great person to ask for help. I may be good at something they struggle with and can help them when it's their turn to edit a paper.

---

[1]   https://www.literaryladiesguide.com/author-quotes/

gwendolyn-brooks-quotes-on-writing-and-life/

[2] https://www.poetryfoundation.org/poets/audre-lorde

Made in the USA
Middletown, DE
20 May 2022

65998355R00040